Two of These and Three of █████████ h

D0469616

Vocabulary

<u>th</u> voiced

1. they
2. their
3. this
4. then
5. the
6. there
7. these
8. those
9. that

<u>th</u> not voiced

10. Smith
11. thin
12. think
13. thick
14. thank
15. three

<u>Story Word</u>

cus tom ers

16. customers

Pam and Ann can help
Mom. They will make
their beds. Then they will
help with the dishes.

Today is pay day.
Pam and Ann will get
their pay.

Pam and Ann waved to Mom. Then they were off to buy some candy!

They ran on the way.
They hoped to get there
fast. Their pay was in
the little blue purse.

7

Pam and Ann got to the store. There was Mr. Smith, the candy man.

"Hello, Mr. Smith," they said. "We came to get a bag of candy."

Mr. Smith said, "So this is pay day for Pam and Ann !"

"What would you like to
buy today ?" asked Mr.
Smith.

Ann put her hand up to the box of gum and said, "I want two of these, please."

Then Ann put her hand
from box to box and
said, "I will take two of
these in this box, and six
of those in that box."

Pam put her hand from box to box and said, "I will take five sticks of this taffy, and three of these chocolate cherries, please."

Thin Mints 6 for 60¢

Pam said, "Let's get some thin mints for Mom. She likes them."

"Dad likes thick mints," said Ann. "I'll get those."

Mr. Smith handed each little girl her bag of candy.

"Thank you, Mr. Smith," said the girls. "Thank **you**," said Mr. Smith.

Pam and Ann left
the store.

Then Mr. Smith turned
to his clerk and said,
"They are my best
customers !"

The End

Bobby Smith Likes Thick Icing

Vocabulary

th not voiced

1. Smith
2. thump
3. think
4. thick
5. thing
6. three
7. both
8. thank

th voiced

9. then
10. them
11. that
12. the
13. mother

Story Word

14. put

(pŏŏt)

Bobby Smith slipped
and fell from the tree.
What a thump!

Thump !   19

"You must stay in bed
and rest," said his mother.

"OK, Mom," Bobby said.

"I think I will bake some cupcakes for you," said Mother. "Your pals may come to see you. Then we can give them some."

"Thank you, Mom," said Bobby. "That will be fun. Will you put thick icing on them ?"

"Yes, I will," said Mom.

Bobby felt a little better that very second !

Mom went to get things set. She made three kinds of icing for the cupcakes: chocolate, vanilla and mint.

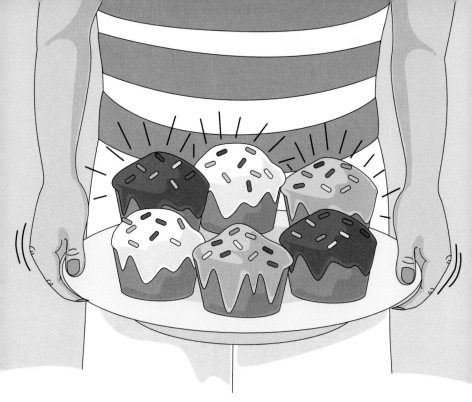

Mom came back with a tray.

"Mmmm," said Bobby. "Three kinds of icing ! I like them all ! And they are so nice and thick ! May I have one, Mom ?"

"Yes, Bobby, you may have one," said Mom. "It may make you feel better."

"You have one, too, Mom, and we will both feel better !" said Bobby.

Bobby's mother smiled.

The End

Vocabulary

1. match
2. catch
3. catcher
4. crutch
5. crutches
6. patch
7. stitch
8. stitches
9. switch
10. pitch
11. pitches
12. pitcher
13. stretch

14. Butch
15. wätch
16. Gretchen

Story Words

be gan
17. began
18. b(oy)
19. boys
pro blem
20. problem
21. n(ow)
22. (out)
23. any time
anytime

Two baseball teams were having a match. One team was the girls' team. One team was the boys' team.

"This will be fun for **us**," said the girls.

"This will be fun for **us**," said the boys.

27

The boys' team had a problem. Their catcher was on crutches. He had a big patch on his leg. The patch was on top of some stitches.

"We can beat the girls' team, anyway," said the coach. "I will let you be catcher, Bobby. You can catch very well. I will switch you to be the first catcher today. You are tall. You can stretch up to catch those pitches."

"Oh, boy!" said Bobby.

The game began. One inning went by. Nobody scored.

Two, then three, then
four innings went by.

Still no score!

Then the girls were up.
Gretchen came to bat.

"Strike one," yelled the
umpire. And then, "Strike
two !" But then...

Watch that ball !
It went over the pitcher,

past the short stop,

and into the back fence !

Gretchen ran to first base,

past second, 35

faster to third

and on home !

Such cheering and yelling !

"Maybe we will win !" they cried.

But the boys had their plans ! "We can't let them beat us," they groaned. "Let's get going !"

"You are up, Bobby!
Let 'em have it!" they
yelled.

Bobby **did**! He hit the
very first pitch, and ran
to first base.

Jimmy struck out, and
so did Mike !

Two outs, and Bobby was
still stuck on first base !

Then Butch smashed one, and did Bobby run !

. . . all the way home !

The next batter struck out. Then it began to rain.

"Oh, no !" said Bobby. "Well, at least the score is tied. You girls just watch ! When our catcher gets off his crutches, we will finish the game and beat you. Just wait and see !"

"Never !" said the girls. "We are a match for you anytime !"

"Don't bet on that !" said Bobby with a smile.

The End

Mitch and His Bean Bag

Vocabulary

1. patch
2. Mitch
3. match
4. matches
5. catch

Story Words

some thing
6. something
him self
7. himself
a way
8. away

Review Vocabulary (ēǿ)

9. bean
10. year
11. jeans
12. each
13. team
14. mean
15. leaf
16. reach
17. reached
18. meat
19. hear
20. clear
21. real
22. streak
23. treat
24. leap
25. leaped
26. fear
27. beast
28. beat
29. near
30. lean

44

Mitch has a little cat.
Her name is Puff. Puff is
one year old.

Mitch has a red bean
bag. He made it himself.
It matches the patch on
his blue jeans.

Mitch and Puff play
with each other. They
make a good team.

Up went Mitch's bean
bag ! Up it went to the
top of the shed !

Puff ran to get the red
bean bag. She did not
see it land on the peak.
Puff ran near the shed.
She saw a red leaf. She
leaped to get it. Puff's
red leaf went way up.
Puff thinks she has a
bean bag, too !

"Puff, you are
something !" said Mitch.
"You can play with a
bean bag, too !"

Puff's bean bag was the
red leaf.

50

Just then a big mean
dog ran up to Puff. Puff
jumped ! In a streak,
Puff was on the peak of
the shed !

Mitch saw Puff up there.
"Do not fear, little Puff,"
said Mitch.

Mitch yelled at the dog.
"Go away, dog! Go
away! Do you hear?"

The big mean dog ran
away fast!

Then Puff saw the bean
bag on the peak of the
shed. She leaned over
to reach it. She gave
it a poke.

The bean bag went sliding. There was Mitch, all set to catch it. And he did !

"Thank you, Puff," said Mitch. "You are the best cat of all! I will give you a dish of meat for a treat."

It was clear to Mitch that Puff was a real pal.

"You are so fast, Puff, you would win in any race!"

Mitch gave her a big hug!

The End

The ABC Code

Vocabulary

1. k̶n̶o̶w̶
2. do̶ors
3. f̄ind
4. wo(er)rd
5. words
6. wo(er)rld
7. story
8. stories
9. finger
10. w̶hole
11. out
12. under
    any place
13. anyplace
    any thing
14. anything
    for ever
15. forever

Review Vocabulary (y=ī)

16. by
17. why
18. try
19. sly
20. spy
21. shy
22. pry
23. sky
24. fry

58

By the time you read
this, your Raceway car
may be speeding on the
Language Arts Raceway
to Step 23 ! Why are
you doing this ? So you
will be a good reader !

When you know the ABC code, no one can take it from you... no matter how much he may try... and even if he is sly, it is yours forever !

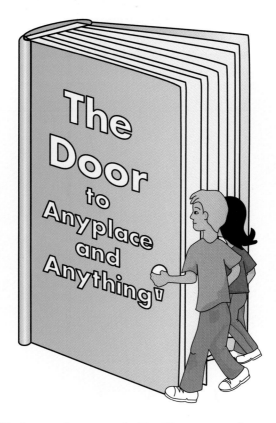

With the ABC code you can read anything you want. There are doors that open to anyplace and anything. Those doors are the covers of books !

You do not have to go to the moon to find out what is there.

You do not have to go under the sea to find out what is there.

You can use the ABC
code to unlock words and
read stories that tell
about anything.

The whole world is at your fingertips. Turn the pages and it will open for you.

The End